CANDLESTICK CHART PATTERNS & INDICATORS FOR BEGGINERS

Understanding Basic Indicators, Understanding Basic Candlestick Charts Patterns

By

Green Ambi

Table of Content

Introduction

This book, CANDLESTICK CHART PATTERNS & INDICATORS FOR BEGGINERS , is dedicated to all forex and crypto dealers, as well as fledgling brokers and amateurs who are interested in learning and trading CHART PATTERNS & INDICATORS FOR BEGGINERS , including old merchants with little experience, taking the necessary steps to win in TRADING rather than giving reasons.

What is a chart pattern?

Day trading chart patterns illustrate price fluctuations over a specific time period. The patterns take on changing shapes depending on what is happening with an item.

Charts show trends.

They help day traders determine whether prices are likely to climb or fall. There are various types of charts in trading.

They all reveal distinct details.
The level of detail required depends on where you're dealing, such as Forex or cryptocurrency marketplaces.

Chart Pattern Basics

How do chart patterns work? Let's start with some basics.

Price movements are represented on charts using trendlines. The shape of the trendline determines whether prices rise or fall.

We identify patterns inside trendlines by examining individual price points along the way.

Day Trading and Chart Patterns

As a day trader, you'll be studying charts constantly.
To aid, let's break down the most fundamental line trends: uptrends and downtrends.

Uptrends are characterized by higher lows and higher "highs".
Downtrends indicate lower "highs" and lower lows.
The simplest patterns are continuations and reversals.

A continuation is a brief pause in which prices continue on the same trajectory as previously.
Reversal patterns arise when a trend shifts and prices move in a new direction.
Let's take a look at some frequent continuation and reversal patterns.

1. Wedges.

Wedges are generated when two trendlines converge. Both lines are going in the same direction, allowing you to draw a wedge or triangle shape.

Down or falling wedges indicate a halt. They frequently precede the transition from a decline to an uptrend.
Up or rising angles indicate an interruption. They could be followed by a reversal.

2. Flags.

Flag patterns appear when there are two parallel trendlines. They can travel upwards, downwards, or horizontally. They frequently indicate a breakout following a consolidation period.

An upslope could indicate a pause, which could reverse a downward trend. A downslope may also indicate an impending shift in an upward trend. Horizontal (pennant) flags typically indicate a continuation of a current trend.

3. Triangles are difficult. However, in layman's words, supply and demand have a significant impact.

Triangles frequently form when supply contracts owing to decreased demand. Shortening supply and decreasing demand eventually combine to generate this triangle pattern. They can also foreshadow a future breakout, so patience may be required.

4. Doubles.

A "double" is usually - but not always - linked with a reversal. It occurs when a price rises or falls twice, encounters resistance, and transitions to a new trending pattern.

Double Top: The price reaches two peaks before it is unable to go any further. It will then reverse down and begin a new pattern.

Double Bottom: The price falls twice before starting to rise again. Learning to recognize such patterns can help day traders make precise, deliberate moves for maximum profit!

5. Head and shoulders.

This chart pattern emerges when there is a major price peak flanked on either side by smaller peaks. So there are three surges, either upward or downward. However, the price eventually rises or falls back to a support level, often known as a "neckline".

Typically, this pattern indicates a reversal of an upward or negative trend.

6. Sushi Rolls

A "sushi roll" develops when you have a specific pattern of inner and outside bars. The "inner" tier consists of bars with a variety of narrow price points. The "outer" layer wraps around these bars, creating a lower low and a higher high.

If you're following a decline, sushi rolls may indicate that it's time to buy.
Sushi rolls may indicate an increase and a good time to sell.
Sushi rolls typically have at least ten bars, but there may be more or less.

Chart patterns that every trader should know

Chart patterns are an important part of technical analysis, but they take considerable practice before they can be used effectively.

To help you understand them, here are ten chart patterns that every trader should be aware of.

Chart Patterns

Head and shoulders.

Double top

Double bottom

Rounding the bottom.

Cup and Handle

Wedges

Pennants or flags

Ascending Triangle

Descending Triangle

Symmetrical triangles

There is no single 'best' chart pattern because they are utilized to indicate different trends in a wide range of markets.

Chart patterns are commonly employed in candlestick trading, making it slightly simpler to see prior market opens and closes.

Some patterns work better in stormy markets than others. Some patterns work best in bullish markets, while others work better in negative markets.

That being said, it is critical to understand the 'optimal' chart pattern for your specific market, since selecting the incorrect one or not knowing which one to utilize may result in a missed opportunity to earn.

Before delving into the complexities of several charts.

Patterns require a brief explanation of support and resistance levels. Support is the point at which the price of an asset stops declining and begins to rise again. Resistance is usually where the price stops climbing and falls back down.

Levels of support and resistance arise as a result of the equilibrium between buyers and sellers, also known as supply and demand.

When there are more buyers than sellers in a market (when demand exceeds supply), prices tend to rise. When there are more sellers than buyers (supply exceeds demand), prices typically decline.

For example, an asset's price could be growing when demand exceeds supply. However, the price will finally reach the highest that buyers are prepared to pay, and demand will decrease at that price level. At this point, buyers might decide to close their positions.

This creates resistance, and the price starts to fall toward a level of support as supply begins to outstrip demand as more and more buyers close their positions.

Once an asset's price falls enough, buyers might buy back into the market because the price is now more acceptable – creating a level of support where supply and demand begin to equal out.

If the increased buying continues, it will drive the price back up towards a level of resistance as demand begins to increase relative to supply.

Once a price breaks through a level of resistance, it may become a level of support.

Types of chart patterns

Chart patterns are typically classified into three types: continuation patterns, reversal patterns, and bilateral patterns.

A continuance indicates that the current trend will continue.
Reversal chart patterns suggest that a trend is likely to shift direction.
Bilateral chart patterns inform traders that the price can move either way, indicating that the market is highly volatile.

You may trade all of these patterns using CFDs. This is because CFDs allow you to go short as well as long, which means you may bet on both falling and rising markets.

You may choose to go short during a bearish reversal or continuation, or long during a bullish reversal or continuation; whether you do so depends on the pattern market analysis that you have carried out.

Learn more about CFDs

The most important thing to remember when using chart patterns as part of your technical analysis, is that they are not a guarantee that a market will move in that predicted direction – they are merely an indication of what might happen to an asset's price.

Head and shoulders.

A head and shoulders chart pattern consists of a high peak flanked by two slightly smaller peaks. Traders use head and shoulders patterns to predict a bullish-to-bearish reversal.

Typically, the first and third peaks are smaller than the second, but they all return to the same level of support, also known as the 'neckline'.

Once the third peak has dropped back to support, it is likely to break into a bearish downtrend.

Double top

A double top is another pattern that traders employ to signal trend reversals. Typically, an asset's price will reach a peak before retreating to a level of support. It will then ascend once more before turning more permanently against the current trend.

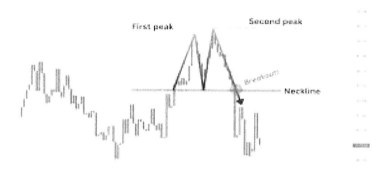

Double bottom

A double bottom chart pattern shows a period of selling in which an asset's price falls below a level of support.

It will then ascend to a point of resistance before descending again. Finally, the trend will reverse and begin to rise as the market becomes more bullish.

A double bottom is a bullish reversal pattern that indicates the conclusion of a downtrend and the start of an uptrend.

Rounding the bottom.

A rounding bottom chart pattern may indicate a continuation or reversal. For example, during an upswing, an asset's price may drop somewhat before rising again. This would represent a bullish continuation.

A bullish reversal rounding bottom, as shown below, occurs when an asset's price is in a downward trend and a rounding bottom forms before the trend reverses and enters a bullish uptrend.

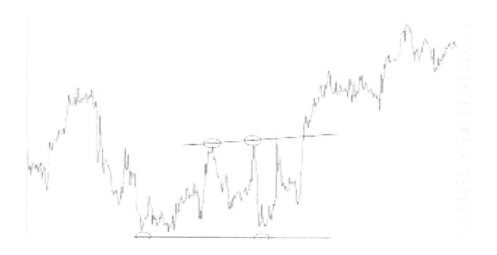

Traders will look to profit from this pattern by purchasing halfway around the bottom, at the low point, and then capitalizing on the continuation after it breaks over a level of resistance.

Cup and Handle

The cup and handle pattern is a bullish continuation pattern that depicts a period of bearish market sentiment before the main trend resumes in a bullish direction.

The cup resembles a rounding bottom chart design, whereas the handle resembles a wedge pattern, as explained in the following section.

Following the rounding bottom, the price of an asset will most likely enter a short retracement, called as the handle since it is limited to two parallel lines on the price graph.

The asset will eventually reverse out of the handle and continue with the overall bullish trend.

Wedges

occur when an asset's price fluctuations constrict between two sloping trend lines. There are two kinds of wedges: rising and falling.

A rising wedge is defined as a trend line sandwiched between two upwardly sloping lines of support and resistance. In this scenario, the line of support is steeper than the resistance line.

This pattern typically indicates that an asset's price will eventually fall more permanently, as indicated when it breaks through the support level.

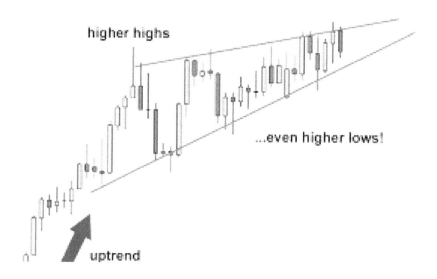

Pennants or flags

Pennant patterns, often known as flags, form after an asset undergoes an uptrend followed by consolidation. Generally, there will be a considerable increase in the early phases of the trend, followed by a succession of smaller upward and downward movements.

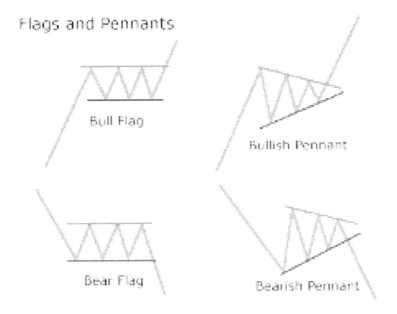

Pennants can be bullish or negative, indicating a continuance or reversal. The above chart illustrates a bullish continuation. In this regard, pennants might be considered a type of bilateral pattern because they exhibit either continuations or reversals.

While a pennant may appear to be similar to a wedge or triangle design (described in the next sections), it is vital to remember that wedges are narrower than pennants or triangles.

Also, wedges differ from pennants in that they are always ascending or descending, whereas pennants are always horizontal.

Ascending Triangle

The ascending triangle is a bullish continuation pattern that indicates the continuation of an upward trend.

To build ascending triangles on charts, first draw a horizontal line along the swing highs (resistance) and then an ascending trend line along the swing lows (support).

Buy stop pending order near the end of the triangle

Ascending triangles frequently have two or more identical peak highs, allowing a horizontal line to be formed.

The trend line denotes the pattern's overall uptrend, whilst the horizontal line represents the asset's historical level of resistance.

Descending Triangle

In contrast, a descending triangle indicates a bearish continuation of a decline. Typically, a trader may take a short position during a descending triangle, possibly using CFDs, in order to profit from a dropping market.

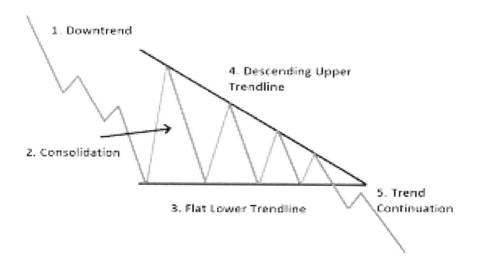

Descending triangles typically shift lower and break through support because they indicate a market dominated by sellers, implying that successively lower peaks are likely to occur and are unlikely to reverse.

Descending triangles are defined by a horizontal line of support and a downward-sloping line of resistance. Eventually, the trend will break through the support and the downturn will resume.

Symmetrical triangles

The symmetrical triangular pattern can be bullish or bearish, depending on the market. In any scenario, it is a continuation pattern, which indicates that after the pattern has formed, the market will typically continue in the same direction as the broader trend.

Symmetrical triangles occur when the price converges on a series of lower peaks and higher troughs.

In the example below, the overall trend is bearish, but the symmetrical triangle indicates that there was a small period of upward reversal.

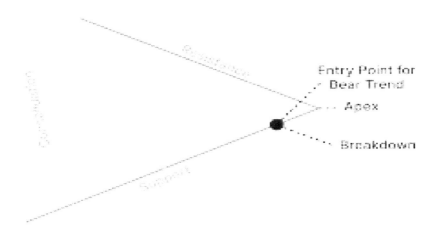

However, if there is no definite trend before the triangle pattern appears, the market may breakout in either way.

This makes symmetrical triangles a bidirectional pattern, which means they are best used in volatile situations where it is unclear which way an asset's price will move.

Main Groups of Chart Patterns

That's a whole lot of chart patterns we just taught you right there.

We're pretty tired so it's time for us to take off and leave it to you from here.. Just playin'! We ain't leaving you till you're ready! In this section, we'll discu a bit more about how to use these chart patterns to your advantage.

It's not enough to just know how the tools work, we've got to learn how to us them.

And with all these new weapons in your arsenal, we'd better get those profits fired up! Let's summarize the chart patterns we just learned and categorize them according to the signals they give.

Reversal Chart Patterns Reversal patterns are those chart formations that signal that the ongoing trend is about to change course.

If a reversal chart pattern forms during an uptrend, it hints that the trend wi reverse and that the price will head down soon. Conversely, if a reversal char pattern is seen during a downtrend, it suggests that the price will move up later on.

We will discussed six chart patterns that provide reversal signals.

I.   Double Top
II.   Double Bottom
III. Head and Shoulders
IV.   Inverse Head and Shoulders
V.   Rising Wedge
VI.   Falling Wedge

Double Top

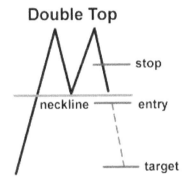

Head and Shoulder

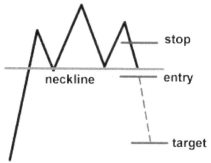

Rising Wedge

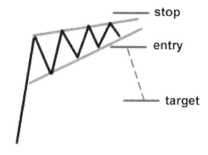

Double Bottom

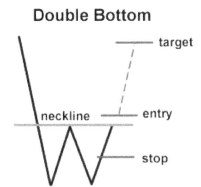

Inverse Head and Sholder

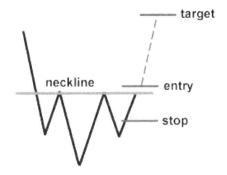

Falling Wedge

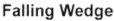

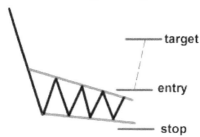

To trade these chart patterns, simply place an order beyond the neckline in the direction of the new trend. Then aim at a target that is roughly the same height as the formation.

For example, if you detect a double bottom, place a long order at the top of the formation's neckline and aim for a target that is the same height as the distance between the bottoms and the neckline.

Don't forget to position your stops to ensure effective risk management! A decent stop loss can be put at the center of the chart formation.

For example, you can measure the distance between the double bottoms and the neckline, split it by two, and use that as the size of your stop.

Continuation Chart Patterns

Continuation chart patterns are chart formations that indicate that an existing trend will resume.

These are commonly referred to as consolidation patterns because they demonstrate how buyers or sellers take a short respite before continuing in the same direction as the previous trend.

Trends rarely go in a straight line upward or downward. They pause and move sideways, "correct" lower or higher, and then regain impetus to resume the main trend.

We have studied various continuation chart patterns, including wedges, rectangles, and pennants. Wedges can be classified as reversal or continuation patterns based on the trend in which they occur.

To trade these patterns, simply place an order above or below the formation (in the direction of the current trend, of course).

Then choose a goal that is at least as large as the wedge and rectangle chart layout.
For pennants, aim higher and target the height of the pennant mast.

Stops in continuation patterns are typically placed above or below the chart formation.

For example, when trading a bearish rectangle, set your stop loss a few pips above the rectangle's top or resistance.

Bilateral Chart Patterns

Bilateral chart patterns are a little trickier because they indicate that the price can move either direction.

Huh? What type of signal is it!

This is a bilateral signal.

This is where triangle formations fit in.

We talked about how the price could break to the upside or downside using triangles?

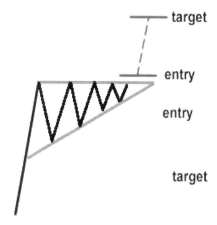

Ascending Triangle

target

entry

entry

target

Descending Triangle

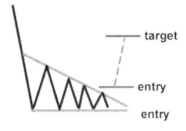

target

entry

entry

target

Symmetrical Triangle

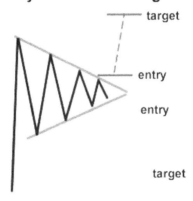

target

entry

entry

target

What Is a Candlestick Pattern?

Candlestick charts are a technical tool that packs data for multiple time frames into single price bars.

This makes them more useful than traditional open, high, low, and close (OHLC) bars or simple lines that connect the dots of closing prices.

Candlesticks build patterns that may predict price direction once completed. Proper color coding adds depth to this colorful technical tool, which dates back to 18th-century Japanese rice traders.

Traditionally, candlesticks are best used on a daily basis, the idea being that each candle captures a full day's worth of news, data, and price action. This suggests that candles are more useful to longer-term or swing traders.

Most importantly, each candle tells a story. When looking at a candle, it's best viewed as a A competition between buyers and sellers.

A light candle (green or white are common defaults) indicates that the buyers won the day, whilst a dark candle (red or black) indicates that the sellers dominated.

What happens between the open and close, and the conflict between buyers and sellers, is what makes candlesticks so appealing as a charting tool.

How To Read a Candlestick Pattern

A daily candlestick depicts a market's opening, high, low, and closing prices (OHLC). The rectangular genuine body, or just body, is colored in a dark color (red or black) for a price decrease and in a light color (green or white) for a price rise.

The lines above and below the body, known as wicks or tails, reflect the day's highest and lowest points.

Taken together, the candlestick's components can frequently foreshadow shifts in a market's direction or highlight large prospective swings that must often be confirmed by the following day's candle.

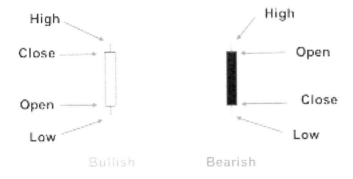

Difference Between Foreign Exchange (FX) Candles and Other Market Candles

Before we go into specific candlestick patterns, let's clarify the distinction between foreign exchange (FX) candlesticks, stock/exchange-traded fund (ETF)/futures, and all other candlesticks.

Because the FX market operates 24 hours a day, the daily closure of one day is usually the opening of the following day.

As a result, there are fewer gaps between price patterns on FX charts. FX candles can only show a gap during the weekend, with the Friday close differing from the Monday open.

Many candlestick patterns rely on price gaps to signal, and those gaps should always be recognized. As for the FX candles, A little imagination is required to identify a potential candlestick indication that does not exactly match the typical candlestick pattern.

For example, in the FX chart below, the bearish engulfing line's body does not completely envelop the previous day's body, but the upper wick does. With a little ingenuity, you'll be able to recognize certain patterns, even if they're not textbook-perfect.

Examples of Candlestick Patterns

The examples below include various candlestick patterns that work remarkably well as price direction and potential reversal indicators.

Each predicts higher or lower costs based on the surrounding price bars. Additionally, they are time sensitive in two ways.

They only work within the parameters of the chart under inspection, whether intraday, daily, weekly, or monthly.

Their potency quickly reduces three to five bars after the pattern is completed. Doji and Spinning Tops

A doji (plural: doji) is a candlestick shape in which the open and closure are identical or nearly so. A spinning top is extremely similar to a doji, but with a very small body. The open and closure are nearly identical.

Both patterns indicate market hesitation, as buyers and sellers have effectively come to an impasse. However, these patterns are extremely essential as indicators that the hesitation will finally pass and a new price direction will emerge.

Below are some visual examples of doji and spinning tops:

Bullish and Bearish Engulfing Lines

An engulfing line is a reliable indicator of a directional change. A bearish engulfing line is a reversal pattern that follows an uptrend.

The secret is that the second candle's body "engulfs" the previous day's body in the reverse direction. This indicates that, in the event of an uptrend, the purchasers made a brief attempt higher but concluded the day considerably below the close of the previous candlestick.

This indicates that the upswing has stalled and has begun to revert lower. Also, take note of the candles from the previous two days, which displayed a double top, also known as a tweezers top, which is a reversal pattern.

A bullish engulfing line is the corollary pattern to a bearish engulfing line and appears after a downward trend. Also, a double bottom, or tweezers bottom, is the corollary formation that suggests a downtrend may be ending and set to reverse higher.

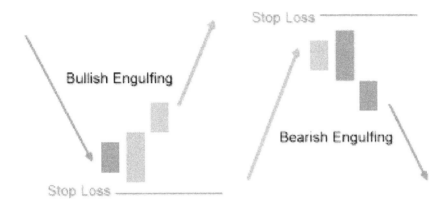

Hammer

A hammer signifies the end of a downward trend. Note the extended lower tail, which suggests that sellers attempted to sell lower but were refused, and the price erased most or all of its losses for the day.

The significant reading is that this is the first time purchasers have emerged in force during the current downtrend, implying a shift in directional mood. The pattern is verified by a bullish candle the next day.

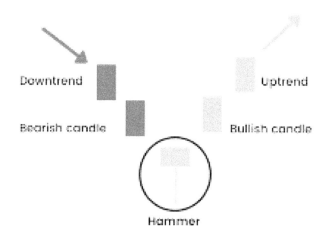

Downtrend

Bearish candle

Uptrend

Bullish candle

Hammer

Hanging Man

A hanging man pattern, which is the corollary to the bullish hammer formation, indicates a significant probable reversal lower. The candle represents the first time in many days that selling interest has entered the market, resulting in the extended tail to the downside.

The buyers fought back, leaving a little, dark body at the top of the candle. The next day's dark candle confirms a short signal.

Abandoned Baby Top or Bottom

An abandoned baby, also known as an island reversal, is a notable pattern that indicates a major reversal in the previous directional movement.

An abandoned baby top emerges after an upswing, whereas an abandoned baby bottom forms after a decline.

The pattern consists of a gap in the direction of the current trend, leaving a candle with a little body (spinning top/or doji) alone at the top or bottom, much like an island.

Confirmation comes on the following day's candle, where a gap lower (abandoned baby top) indicates that the previous gap higher has been erased and selling interest has arisen as the dominant market force.

The following day, confirmation is accompanied with a long, black candle.

Take Special Note to Long Tails and Small Bodies.

Candlesticks with a small body, such as a doji, suggest that buyers and sellers were unable to reach an agreement, resulting in the close being practically identical to the opening. (Such a candlestick might alternatively have a very small body, resulting in a spinning top.)

Small bodies show the market's ambivalence about its current course.

This shows that such little bodies are frequently reversal signs, implying that the directional movement (up or down) has run out of steam.

Take careful notice of important hesitation candles, as either the bulls or the bears will win out in the end. This is a moment to sit back and study the price behavior, remaining ready to act when the market shows its hand.

Another key candlestick signal to watch out for are long tails, especially when they're combined with small bodies. Long tails represent an unsuccessful effort of buyers or sellers to push the price in their favored direction, only to fail and have the price return to near the open.

Just such a pattern is the doji shown below, which signifies an attempt to move higher and lower, only to finish out with no change. This comes after a move higher, suggesting that the next move will be lower.

Which Candlestick Pattern is the Most Reliable?

Many patterns are preferred and regarded as the most dependable by certain traders. Some of the most common patterns include bullish/bearish engulfing lines, bullish/bearish long-legged doji, and bullish/bearish abandoned baby top and bottom.

In the interim, various neutral potential reversal indications, such as doji and spinning tops, will arise, alerting you to the next directional move.

Does Candlestick Pattern Analysis Actually Work?

Yes, candlestick analysis can be useful provided you follow the guidelines and wait for confirmation, which usually appears in the next day's candle.

Candlestick analysis is used by traders all around the world, particularly in Asia, to determine general market direction rather than where prices will be in the next two to four hours.
This is why daily candles work best Instead, use shorter-term candlesticks.

How Can You Read a Candle Pattern?

A candle pattern is best understood by determining if it is bullish, bearish, or neutral. Watching a candlestick pattern form can be time-consuming and aggravating.

If you notice a pattern and receive confirmation, you have a foundation for making a transaction. Be careful not to see patterns where none exist. Allow the market to do its thing, and you will ultimately receive a high-probability candlestick indication.

How Do Candlesticks Form on a Trading Chart?

Candlesticks are like an X-ray of the market. You can see what's going on beneath the surface, such as shifts in market strength and direction, as well as how emotions influence patterns.

Each candlestick displays price information over a certain time period, such as one trading day in a daily chart, one hour in an hourly chart, and so on.

shift the time window on a chart, and the candlesticks will shift correspondingly. Next, we'll look at the components of candlesticks to see how they're formed and what they symbolize.

Candlestick Components

A candlestick has four components: the open, close, high, and low prices for a given time period. Let us look at an example.

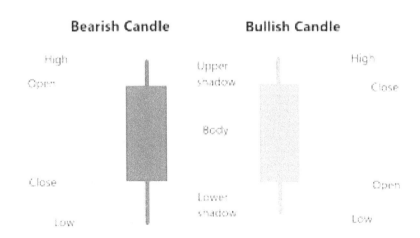

What is the Three Outside Up candlestick pattern?

The three outside up is a pattern that forms on the candlestick chart over three trading sessions. Three outside up comprises three candlesticks and forms typically in a downtrend or an uptrend an extended downward price swing. Here it can indicate a potential price reversal to the upside.

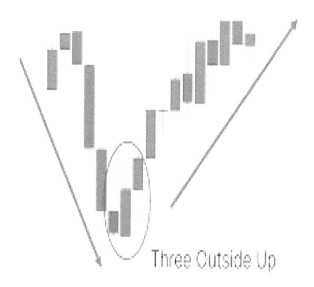

Three Outside Up

This triple candlestick pattern is an extension of the bullish reversal day pattern or the bullish engulfing pattern. This pattern is formed over three days of trading after a prolonged down string on the daily timeframe with the first two trading days looking like a bullish reversal or bullish engulfing day formation.

The third candlestick completing the pattern is a bullish candlestick that approves the potential reversal.

In the above figure, we can see the schematic diagram of the three outside up patterns. We have three consecutive candlesticks here as mentioned above.

The three outside up candlestick patterns frequently occur and serve as a reliable indicator of a trend in reversal. Traders use it as a primary buying or selling signal.

One can observe that The first candle continues to exhibit a negative trend. The first candle closes lower than it opens. This suggests a short-selling interest because it boosts confidence in the market's bearish movement. The second candle will open lower than the first.

Because of its extended true body, it will appear to reverse the chart's orientation. It demonstrates bullishness as the candle passes the first candle's initial tick. This behavior raises one red flag for any bears looking to take profits and tighten their stops in anticipation of a market reversal.

The third candle provides more indication that the market's trends may reverse. This occurs because the security's price rises significantly over the borders of the first candle, indicating gains.

The third candle completes the bullish candlestick, known as a 'outside day'. The trading day ends after the trader observes all three candles.

There is an increase in bullish confidence, which triggers any purchase indications. This is because the asset closes at a new high on the third candlestick.

How are three outside-up candlesticks formed?

The three outside up candlestick is formed when the two occurrences of a bullish candlestick, the one that closes higher than it opened a bearish candlestick, the one that closes lower than it opened follows.

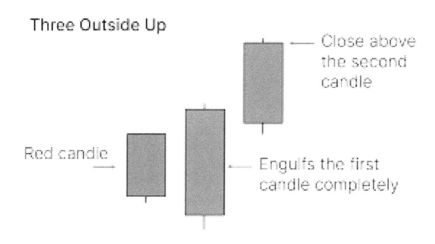

Three successive candlesticks particularly form the three outside up patterns. Usually, this appears after a bearish trend. The movement of the candles indicates whether a trend reversal is imminent or not.

Below we have mentioned the formation of the pattern. The market has to decline for the three outside up patterns to appear. The first candle of the pattern will be red.

This signifies a downward trend. It will form a large green candle. It will be long enough so that it can contain the first candle within its true body. The third or final candle indicating three outside up has to be green again.

However, this candle must close higher than the second one. This depicts that the downward trend is changing direction.

What does the Green Three Outside Up Candlestick indicate?

Green three outside up candlestick design consists of green candlesticks. The pattern signals an upcoming uptrend due to the strong buying pressure. These candlesticks do not possess long shadows and these open within the real body of the previous candle in this pattern.

How Important is the Color of the Three Outside Up Candlestick?
The colors of the candles have great significance in three outside up candlestick patterns. The first candle is one short-bodied red candle.

This is so because there is in-fighting that is going on among the bulls and bears when the first candle forms. There has to be a prevailing downtrend for the trend to appear.

The second one is a large green candle signifying that the situation is now in control of the bulls. The first candle must accommodate within the body of the second green candle.

The second candle is an enveloping one. This supports the bulls' ability to take control and overcome the bears from this point forward. This condition signals a positive reversal rise.

The third green candle signals an imminent bullish reversal trend. It is more tightly closed than the second one. The third candle must shut higher than the second. Actually, the third candle initiates a bullish reversal.

When does Three Outside Up Candlestick occur?
When we look at the three trading sessions that make up the pattern, we can observe that the first day concludes with a small bearish candlestick.

It actually shows that the bearers are becoming weary, but it appears to be a continuation of the downswing. The diminishing momentumof the bears emboldens the bulls to set up and also take control.

A long bullish engulfing candlestick formed the following trading day confirms this. This huge candlestick tells something about the shifting of market sentiments.

After a long era of bear dominance, the bulls are retaking control and beginning to dominate. This indicates an upward price rise in the near future. The bulls continue to dominate on the third trading day. This confirms that the bulls have taken control of the market's direction.

How frequently does Three Outside Up Candlestick occur?

The three outside up candlestick pattern happens regularly and is a good indicator of a reversal. Despite its popularity, the design does not necessarily result in a high profit margin. You can make a net profit of approximately 5% on average over the long term, as per statistical data.

How can you read Three Outside Up Candlesticks in Technical Analysis?

A daily candlestick depicts the opening, high, low, and closing prices of a market. The rectangular genuine body is dark (red or black) when the price is reduced and light (white or green) when the price is increased.

The lines below and above the body are known as tails or wicks. They reflect the highest and lowest points of a certain day.

The portions of the candlestick used in technical analysis might signify frequent changes in the direction of a market or show big potential moves that will be witnessed by the candle the following day.

The following conditions must be met for the pattern to form properly.

The pattern must form during a prolonged downswing.
The second session's open price is less than the first session's close price.
The second session's candlestick has a higher close price than the first session's candlestick.
The close price of the third session's candlestick is higher than the close price of the previous session.
This pattern's power grows in proportion to the magnitude of the enveloping second candle. The size of the engulfing second candlestick in contrast to the first bearish candlestick will determine the significance of the pattern.

How reliable are the Three Outside Up Candlesticks in Technical Analysis? The three Outside Up patterns serve as a reliable indicator of a reversal in a trend. Traders use it as a primary buying and selling signal.

Traders use this signal in the context of other indicators. This pattern is best for relatively short holding periods and is useful mostly for short-term trading Though often found, the pattern does not always give a good profit margin.

The pattern does not necessarily mean that the market's direction has been confirmed. One should search for a larger market movement than this short-term indicator. When setting stop losses or booking profits, it's usually a good idea to couple the indicator with others.

When is the ideal moment to trade utilizing the Three Outside Up Candlestick?

The optimal time frame for the three outside up candlestick is a brief holding period of 1 to 10 days, with daily bars. The most popular time frames for trading are the 15-minute and 5-minute candlestick charts.

How Do I Trade With Three Outside Up Candlesticks in the Stock Market?

The practice of trading with three outside-up patterns using a diagram.

Before trading an asset, a trader should first confirm the overall market conditions. A trader should not commit to any position until he or she receives confirmation from other indicators.

When a trader is confident in his or her trading abilities, he or she should confirm the pattern. The three candlestick rising pattern is formed when three candlesticks form at the end of an existing bearish trend.

The trader purchases the stock precisely above the high of the third candle. This is only done with the fourth candle. i.e. the candle that follows the third candle in the pattern.

Traders can take profits when the price exceeds a 1:2 risk/reward ratio or a predetermined profit % target. Traders can alternatively wait till the trend breaks.

Where is the Three Outside Up symbol usually used?

Traders use the Three Outside Up indication as their primary buying or selling signal. This is quite useful in swing trading. One must grasp how to apply it efficiently in diverse market scenarios.

Is the Three Outside Up pattern in an uptrend a sell signal?

No, three outside up in an uptrend does not indicate a sell signal. One can see that the first candle continues to exhibit a negative trend. The first candle closes lower than it opens. This suggests a short selling interest.

because it boosts confidence in the market's gloomy trend. The second candle will open lower than the first.

However, due to its extended true body, it will appear to reverse the chart's orientation. It demonstrates bullishness as the candle passes the first candle's initial tick.

This behavior raises one red flag for any bears looking to take profits and tighten their stops in anticipation of a market reversal. This moves the price above the range of the first candle.

This occurs because the security appears again with the price well above the borders of the first candle. This concludes a bullish outside day candlestick. Increasing bull confidence triggers buying signals. This was confirmed when security posted a new high on the third candle.

Benefits of the Three Outside Up Candlestick Pattern?

Traders prefer this pattern for technical analysis due to the benefits listed below.

One candlestick symbolizes any time period of an item, hence it is infinitely adaptable.

Lots of information: They are quite an exact and pure style of charting that simply displays the data in an easy-to-understand and appealing way because these candlesticks indicate opens, closes, highs, and lows of a specific time span.

Simple to understand: The candlestick chart simplifies the analysis of price data. You can easily come up with a trading plan. They are artistically beautiful, with configurable outline and color options.

Indicators: Maximum indicators work wonderfully with the three outside-up candlestick patterns.

Market psychology and sentiment: Candlestick charts are an excellent way to depict market mood over a specific time period. Traders can use numerous candlestick patterns, such as Doji patterns, to determine the general bias over a certain time period.

Traders regard the three outside up patterns as a solid indication; nevertheless, confirmation from other indicators serves as an added benefit when entering a trade.

What are the disadvantages of the Three Outside Up Candlestick?

The three outside up patterns have constraints, six of which are listed below.

Too much information: Not all trading techniques are identical. Some techniques can gain an advantage by eliminating the noise of standard trading systems and focusing on only one or two elements present in The chart. As a result, candlesticks will clutter the charts in such trading strategies.

Not always accurate: Despite its prevalence, the pattern does not always result in a high profit margin. The pattern does not necessarily mean that the market's direction has been confirmed.

One should search for a larger market movement than this short-term indicator. When setting stop losses or booking profits, it's usually a good idea to couple the indicator with others.

Difficult to identify: Unless a bar form is watched retroactively in real time, traders will have no notion which came first, the low or the high.

They must go back to the lower time periods to investigate what occurred within that candlestick. A bullish bar on a higher period indicates an overarching trend on lower time frames, but it can also signify a single parabolic surge.

Gaps: Candlestick charts contain gaps. Also, there are times when a candle shuts at a specific level and the next candle opens at a different level.

Apophenia: Our brain wants to see patterns while also looking for meaning. When combined with technical analysis, we frequently notice patterns in random things and try to attach things where there is nothing to the said data. Candlesticks are often known for this trip.

False confidence: Many of us are often tricked to believe in one-dimensional trading systems using only the price data. This is because the candlestick chart makes price data understanding very easy. You can effortlessly formulate a strategy to trade it.

The restrictions listed above indicate that the outside up signal is not infallible and should be used in conjunction with other indicators.

What is the opposite of three outside-up candlesticks?

The three outside down candlestick pattern is the inverse of the three outside up pattern, and it typically appears during a bullish trend.

The first candle continues the bullish trend, with the closure higher than the open. This shows high buying interest, which boosts bull confidence. The second candle opens higher, but then reverses and crosses through the initial tick, indicating bear power.

This price movement advises bulls to tighten stops or take profits, as a reversal is possible. The security continues to report losses, with its price dropping below the first candle's range. This completes a bearish outside day candlestick. Now, this increases bear confidence setting off a selling signal.

What candlestick pattern is similar to the Three Outside Up Candlestick?

Similar to the three outside up candlestick pattern, the three inside up pattern is a bullish reversal pattern. It consists of one enormous down candle, one smaller up candle trapped within the previous candle, and another up candle that closes once the second candle has closed.

Is the Three Outside Up pattern a bullish reversal?

Yes, the three outside up is a three-candle reversal pattern shown on a candlestick chart. It is a bullish candlestick pattern that appears near the end of a downtrend.

What's the difference between Three Outside Up and Three Outside Down?

Outside Up and Down are three-candle reversal patterns that appear on candlestick charts.

The patterns need three candles to form in a particular sequence that the current trend has lost momentum and can signal a reversal of an existing trend. The pattern forms when a bearish candlestick is followed by two cases of a bullish candlestick or vice versa.

The three outside up is a bullish candlestick pattern with the following features.

The market is in downturn.
The foremost candle is bearish.
And the second candle is bullish, with a long actual body that completely contains the first candle.
The third candle here is bullish, with a higher closing than the second candle.
The three outside down is a bearish candlestick pattern with the following qualities.

The market is on an ascent.
The foremost candle is bullish.
And the second candle is bearish, with a long genuine body that completely covers the first candle.
The third candle here is bearish, with a lower closure than the second candle.

Because the second candle engulfs the first candle, it signals the end of the current trend. The third candle illustrates the acceleration of the reversal.

Both the three Outside Up and three Outside Down patterns occur frequently and traders see them as trustworthy indicators of a reversal. They employ these indicators as primary sell or buy signals.

Indicators Analysis

Whether you're interested in forex trading, commodities trading, or stock trading, incorporating technical analysis into your technique, which involves understanding several trading indicators, can be beneficial.

Trading indicators are mathematical computations that appear as lines on a price chart and can assist traders in identifying specific signals and market trends.

There are several sorts of trading indicators, including leading and lagging indicators. A leading indicator forecasts future price changes, whereas a lagging indicator examines historical trends and suggests momentum.

In general, technical indicators fall into five categories: trend, mean reversion, relative strength, volume, and momentum.

Leading indicators seek to predict where the price will go, whilst lagging indicators provide a historical record of the background factors that led to the current price.

Bollinger bands, stochastics, and on-balance volume (OBV) are some of the most used technical indicators.

Technical indicators provide insight into support and resistance levels, which can be useful in developing a low risk-reward ratio approach.

Beginner Trading Strategies:

When creating their first trading screens, most amateurs follow the crowd, grabbing a stack of prepackaged indicators and shoving as many as possible beneath the price bars of their preferred equities.

This "more is better" strategy stifles signal production by looking at the market from too many perspectives at once. It's paradoxical because indicators perform best when they simplify the analysis, cutting through the noise and offering useful information on trend, momentum, and timing.

Instead, you might take a different approach by categorizing the types of information you want to track throughout the market day, week, or month. Almost all technical indicators are classified into five types of research.

Each group can be further separated into leading and lagging. Leading indicators attempt to predict where the price is headed while lagging indicators offer a historical report of background conditions that resulted in the current price being where it is.

Trend indicators (lagging) determine if a market is trending upward, downward, or sideways over time.

Mean reversion indicators (lagging) determine how far a price swing will extend before a counter-impulse causes a pullback.

Relative strength indicators (leading) detect fluctuations in purchasing and selling pressure.

Momentum indicators (leading) measure the rate of price change over time. Volume indicators (leading or trailing) add up trades to determine whether bulls or bears are in charge.

So, how does a newbie select the appropriate setting from the start and save months of unproductive signal production? In most circumstances, the ideal way is to start with the most popular figures and modify one indicator at a time to determine if the results improve or degrade your performance. Using this strategy, you'll soon understand the precise requirements of your level.

Now that you've learned the five ways that indicators analyze market activity, let's look at the finest ones in each category for new traders.

Trend Indicators: 50-Day and 200-Day EMAs

We'll begin with two indicators that are displayed in the same panel as the daily, weekly, and intraday price bars. Moving averages analyze price movement over certain time periods and divide the total to generate a running average that is updated with each new bar.

The 50- and 200-day exponential moving averages (EMAs) are more responsive versions of their well-known counterparts, simple moving averages (SMAs).

In a nutshell, the 50-day EMA monitors the average intermediate price of a security, and the 200-day EMA measures the average long-term price.

In the preceding example, the 50- and 200-day EMAs increased consistently over the summer. The 50-day EMA fell in August, and the 200-day EMA followed suit a month later. The short-term average then crossed over the longer-term average (indicated by the red circle), signifying a bearish change in trend that preceded a historic breakdown.

Note that this example is the historical price action of a U.S. Oil fund.

Mean Reversion Indicators

Bollinger Bands can reveal concealed buying and selling impulses, triggering counter-waves or retracements. Bollinger bands (20, 2) attempt to identify these turning events by evaluating how far price can deviate from a central tendency pivot—the 20-day SMA in this case—before initiating a reversionary impulse move back to the mean.

The bands also contract and extend in response to volatility changes, indicating to observant traders when this hidden force is no longer an impediment to rapid price movement.

Relative Strength Indicators

Stochastics

Market activity occurs in buy-and-sell cycles, which can be spotted using stochastics (14,7,3) and other relative strength indicators.
These cycles frequently peak at overbought or oversold levels before reversing direction, with the two indicator lines crossing over.

Cycle changes do not invariably result in greater or lower security prices, as one might think. Rather, bullish or bearish turns indicate periods when buyers or sellers have control of the ticker tape. Price change continues to be driven by volume, momentum, and other market variables.

SPDR S&P Trust (SPY) oscillates through a succession of buy-and-sell cycles during a five-month period.

Look for signals in which:

A crossing happened at or around an overbought or oversold level.

Indicator lines are then pushed toward the center of the display. In highly trending markets, stochastics can swing around extreme levels for long periods of time, necessitating two-tier confirmation.

And, while 14,7,3 is an excellent option for new traders, experiment to discover the setting that best suits the instrument you're evaluating. For example, skilled traders use faster 5,3,3 inputs.

Momentum Indicators

MACD

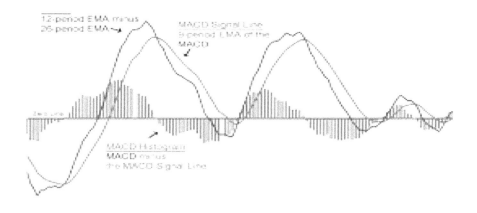

The Moving Average Convergence Divergence (MACD) indicator, set at 12, 26, and 9, provides inexperienced traders with a strong tool for analyzing quick price changes.

This basic momentum indicator evaluates how quickly a market is moving and attempts to identify natural turning moments. When the histogram hits a peak and then reverses course to cross the zero line, buy or sell signals are generated.

The height or depth of the histogram, as well as the rate of change, combine to produce a wide range of important market data.

SPY exhibits four distinct MACD signals during a five-month period. The first signal indicates decreasing momentum, whereas the second catches a directed shove that occurs immediately after the signal is triggered.

The third signal appears to be fake reading but accurately predicts the end of the February–March buying impulse. The fourth triggers a whipsaw that's evident when the histogram fails to penetrate the zero line.

Volume Indicators

On-Balance-Volume (OBV)

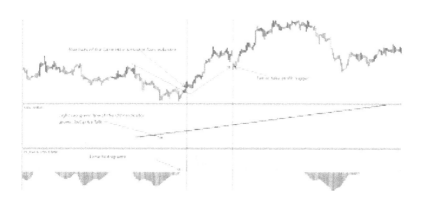

Keep volume histograms beneath your price bars to assess current levels of interest in a specific asset or market. The slope of involvement over time suggests new trends, frequently before price patterns complete breakouts or breakdowns.

You can also run a 50-day volume average over the indicator to evaluate how the current session compares to previous activity.

To complete your transaction flow snapshot, include on-balance volume (OBV), which is an accumulation-distribution indicator. The indicator calculates buying and selling activity to determine if bulls or bears are winning the struggle for higher or lower prices.

On OBV, you may draw trendlines and keep track of the highs and lows in order. It performs exceptionally well as a convergence-divergence technique. For instance, from January to April, Bank of America (BAC) proved this when prices hit a higher high while OBV hit a lower high, signaling a bearish divergence preceding a steep decline.

Support and Resistance Levels

Support is a price level at which a security tends to stop dropping and possibly rebound back, indicating a concentration of buying demand. In contrast, resistance is a level at which a security frequently stops its upward progress, indicating a concentration of selling interest.

These levels are noteworthy because they reflect the aggregate activities of market participants.

As a new trader, it's vital to identify support and resistance using historical price data, as some levels have regularly served as turning points. The technical indications mentioned above can help to improve the reliability of the levels you've found.

There are also unique considerations for beginners who may prefer lesser risk-reward trade-offs. In general, buying at a strong support level The risk-reward ratio is positive, as the anticipation is for an upward bounce.

On the other hand, selling or shorting around a strong resistance level enables traders to profit from the expected decline. Keep these tactics in mind while you work with the technical indications we mentioned before.

Fibonacci Retracement.

Fibonacci retracement is a powerful tool in every trader's toolset, especially for newcomers looking to comprehend market movements.

Fibonacci retracement is named after the famed Italian mathematician Leonardo Fibonacci. It is based on a sequence of numbers, each of which is the sum of the two numbers before it.

In trading, Fibonacci retracement is used to identify probable support and resistance levels by drawing horizontal lines at significant Fibonacci levels, such as 23.6%, 38.2%, 50%, 61.8%, and 78.6%.

These levels are regarded notable because they frequently correspond to natural market retracement levels during price corrections within a larger trend.

In an uptrend, the tool is applied from low to high, and in a downtrend, it is applied from high to low.
Once these levels are charted, traders watch for potential reversal points, where the price may bounce or slow down in its present trend.

Most significantly, the 50% level is not a Fibonacci number, but it is frequently used in the tool as a psychological marker symbolizing the midway point of the retracement.

Which Indicator is Best for Recognizing Trend Reversals?

Moving averages, particularly the EMA, are often employed to detect trend reversals.

When a shorter-term moving average crosses above a longer-term one, it indicates a possible uptrend, but a cross below may imply a downturn, assisting novice traders in identifying trend changes.

What Are the Most Important Considerations When Using Bollinger Bands for Trading?

Bollinger Bands are effective for detecting volatility and probable reversals. They are divided into three bands: middle (SMA), upper (SMA + standard deviation), and lower (SMA - standard deviation).

When prices touch the upper band, it may suggest overbought situations, whilst touching the lower band may indicate oversold conditions, assisting novice traders in making decisions.

Is volume an important consideration in technical analysis?

Volume is an important aspect in technical analysis, as it indicates the strength of price fluctuations. Novice traders should pay attention to volume spikes that accompany price movements, as they confirm the seriousness of the shift.

Which Mistakes Should Novice Traders Avoid When Using Technical Indicators?

Novice traders may be more prone to overcomplicating methods, relying entirely on indicators without considering the larger market backdrop, and ignoring risk management.

Part of the process of becoming a more experienced trader is developing a well-rounded trading strategy that includes several indicators and specific actions to take.

Effective Exit Trading Strategies

Traders spend hours fine-tuning entrance techniques just to blow out their accounts with disastrous exits. In fact, most of us lack adequate exit strategies resulting in being shook out at the lowest possible price.

We can correct this error by employing traditional tactics that can increase profitability.

Before we get into the techniques, let's take a look at why the holding time is vital. Then we'll look at the mistaken concept of market timing, followed by stop and scaling procedures that protect profits and limit losses.

Many traders develop effective exit plans but fail to implement them when the time comes; the consequences can be disastrous.

When developing your strategy, begin by estimating the reward and risk levels before entering a trade, and then utilize those levels as a guide to exit the position at the optimum price, whether you're earning or losing.

Market timing, a frequently misunderstood concept, can be an effective exit strategy when handled appropriately.

Stop-loss and scaling strategies also allow intelligent, systematic investors to protect earnings while reducing losses.

Holding Periods

It's hard to discuss exits without mentioning the value of a holding period that works nicely with your trading approach. The magic time frames roughly correspond with the overall technique chosen to withdraw money from the financial markets:

Day trading: from minutes to hours.
Swing Trading: Hours to Days.
Position Trading: Days to Weeks.
Investment timeframe: weeks to months
Choose the category that most closely matches your market strategy, as this will determine how long you have to book your profit or loss. Stick to the rules, or you risk converting a trade into an investment and a momentum play into a scalp. This strategy necessitates discipline because certain positions perform so well that you want to keep them beyond the time limit.

While you can stretch and squeeze a holding period to account for market conditions, taking your exit within parameters builds confidence, profitability, and trading skill.

Market Timing:

Develop the practice of setting reward and risk targets before joining any transaction. Look at the chart to determine the next resistance level that is likely to come into action within the time restrictions of your holding period.

That indicates the reward target. Then find the price at which you will be proven incorrect if the security rotates and hits it.

That is your risk target. Now, compute the reward/risk ratio, aiming for at least 2:1 in your favor. Anything less, and you should avoid the deal and look for a better opportunity.

Concentrate trade management on the two primary exit prices. Assume things are going well for you and the increasing price is approaching your reward target. The price rate of change now comes into play, because the faster it approaches the magic amount, the more options you have for a favorable exit.

Your first choice is to take a blind exit at the current price, congratulate yourself on a job well done, and move on to the next trade.

When the price is strongly trending in your favor, it is advisable to allow it to exceed the reward objective and place a protective stop at that level while attempting to increase winnings. Then look for the next obvious barrier, and stay

Positioned as long as it does not violate your hold period.

Slow advances are more difficult to trade because numerous securities will approach but not meet the reward threshold. This necessitates a profit protection technique that kicks in moment the price has covered 75% of the difference between your risk and reward targets.

Set a trailing stop to protect partial winnings, or, if you're trading in real time, keep one finger on the exit button while watching the ticker. The trick is to hold your position until price movement provides you a cause to exit.

Stop Loss Strategies

Stops must go where they can get you out when a security breaches the technical reason you entered the trade. This is a perplexing concept for traders who have been taught to set stops based on arbitrary amounts, such as a 5% drawdown or $1.50 below the opening price.

These placements make no sense because they are not tailored to the peculiarities and volatility of the specific instrument. Instead, employ violations of technical features such as trendlines, round numbers, and moving averages to determine the logical stop-loss price.

The ensuing bounce returns to the high, prompting the trader to take a long position in expectation of a breakout.

Common sense implies that a trendline break will invalidate the rally thesis, necessitating an instant departure. In addition, the 20-day simple moving average (SMA) has aligned with the trendline, increasing the likelihood that a breach will result in increased selling pressure.

Modern markets necessitate an extra stage in efficient stop placement. Algorithms now routinely target common stop-loss levels, shaking off retail players before resuming trading across support or resistance.

This necessitates placing stops away from the numbers indicating that you are incorrect and must leave. Finding the optimal price to avoid these stop runs is more art than science.

As a In average, an additional 10 to 15 cents should work for a low-volatility transaction, however an additional 50 to 75 cents may be required for a momentum play.

When watching in real time, you have more options because you can withdraw at your initial risk objective and re-enter if the price returns to the contested level.

Scaling Exit Strategies

For a scalable exit strategy, raise your stop to break even as soon as a fresh trade turns a profit. This can boost confidence because you now have a free trade.

Then sit back and let it run until the price reaches 75% of the risk-reward gap. You then have the choice of exiting all at once or in chunks.

This choice considers position size as well as the strategy being used. For example, breaking up a tiny deal into even smaller sections makes no sense; instead, look for the best time to dump the entire stake or use the stop-at-reward technique.

Larger positions benefit from a tiered exit plan The first third is at 75% of the distance between risk and reward targets, whereas the second third is at the target itself.

Place a trailing stop behind the third piece after it has passed the goal, and use that level as a rock-bottom exit if the position turns south. Over time, you'll discover that this third item is a lifesaver, typically yielding a significant profit.

Finally, examine one exception to this tiering technique. Sometimes the market gives out gifts, and it is our responsibility to select the low-hanging fruit.

So, when a news shock creates a significant gap in your direction, exit the entire position swiftly and without regret, remembering the old adage: never look a gift horse in the mouth.

Pullbacks

Let's go over the most favorable technical conditions for a pullback to turn on a dime the moment you take a risk in the opposite direction. First, you must detect a strong enough trend to ensure that other pullback players are lined up just behind you, ready to join in and transform your idea into a consistent profit.

In other words, take advantage of market psychology and let others help out. Securities that reach new highs or drop to new lows can meet this condition if they move well beyond a technical breakthrough or breakdown level.

An upswing to a peak or a bear trend to a trough is noticeable, particularly on higher-than-normal volume. It's also ideal when the trending security reverse quickly after topping or bottoming out without building a sizable consolidation or trading range. This is needed because the intervening range will limit the profit potential during the subsequent bounce or rollover.

Example: Microsoft

Assume ABC Corp. shares had been trading inside a three-month range before breaking out on above-average volume. It pauses for a week before selling off, giving up roughly half of the previous uptrend, and finds firm support at the breakout level and 50-day EMA.

A noon turnaround produces a modest Doji candlestick, indicating a reversal, which gains traction a few days later, pushing more than two points into a test of the previous high. The stock then maintains its robust ascent, setting several multi-year highs.

Finding the Perfect Entry Price.

Once the pullback begins, keep an eye out for cross-verification. This term refers to tight price zones where multiple types of support or resistance align, favoring a quick reversal and a strong push in the direction of the dominant trend.

When this zone is tightly squeezed and multiple types of support or resistance align exactly, the chances of a bounce or rollover increase.

For example, a sell-off to a breakout through horizontal highs that coincides with a crucial Fibonacci retracement and an intermediate moving average, such as the 50-day EMA, increases the likelihood of a successful pullback trade.

Nonetheless, you can enter pullbacks in less favorable circumstances by scaling into opposing price levels, addressing support and resistance Instead of thin lines, consider price bands.

Example

Assume that XYZ stock carves out a nine-month trading range before going vertical in a high volume breakout after a well-known hedge fund manager joins the company.

The news triggers a massive one-day gain, followed by an immediate drop that finds fresh support near the top of the range, now exactly lined with the 62% Fibonacci retracement and 50-day EMA. The stock turns on a dime and resumes its ascent at a slower speed. It hits a six-year high two months later.

Opportunistic Profits

Take aggressive profits upon trade entrance or scale-out, pocketing cash as the security regains lost ground.

Place Fibonacci grids over a) the last wave of the primary trend and b) the whole pullback wave to tailor risk management to the retracement pattern's features. This combination can indicate harmonic price levels when the two grids align, indicating hidden obstacles.

Gaps and narrow trading ranges should also be monitored for counter swings, as retreat plays always run the danger of printing lower highs in uptrends and higher lows in downtrend.

In most circumstances, the best exits will occur when the market swings quickly in your direction into a visible barrier, such as the last major swing high in an Uptrend or swing low in a downtrend.

Example

Acme, Inc. broke its 19-month support in November, coinciding with lower crude oil prices. The high volume decrease bottoms out a few weeks later, allowing for a retreat that stalls at the 38% Fibonacci sell-off retracement, presenting a low-risk short sale pullback entry.

A second retracement grid put over the pullback wave aids in trade management by identifying natural zones where the decline may stall or reverse. The bull hammer reversal at the 78.6% retracement in January signaled that short-sellers could be targeted, implying a quick exit to safeguard profits.

Effective Stop Loss Strategies

Losing trades with pullback plays are usually due to one of three factors. First, you underestimate the magnitude of the countertrend wave and enter too soon. Second, you enter at the optimal price, but the countertrend persists, disrupting the logical mathematics that triggered your entry signals.

Third, the bounce or rollover starts but then stops, crossing the entry price since your risk management strategy failed. The final scenario is the easiest to handle. Place a trailing stop behind your position as soon as it moves in your favor, and modify it as your profit grows.

The stop required when you first enter the position is proportional to the price set for entrance. As you gain experience, you'll find that many pullbacks contain logical entries at many levels.

The more you wait and the deeper you go without breaching the technicals, the easier it is to set a stop only a few ticks or cents below a significant cross-verification level. A deep entry approach will miss perfect reversals at intermediate levels, but it will result in the highest returns and the fewest losses.

If you decide to take numerous shots at intermediate levels, you should limit the position size and apply stops at arbitrary loss levels, such as 25- to 50-cent exposure on a blue chip and one- to two-dollar exposure on a high beta stock, such as a junior biotech or China play.

Conclusion

The first rule of trading indicators is that you should never employ an indicator alone or combine too many indications at once.

Concentrate on a handful that you believe will be most effective for your goals. You should also employ technical indicators in conjunction with your own analysis of an asset's price fluctuations over time (the 'price action').

It's crucial to remember that you must confirm a signal in some way. If you receive a 'buy' signal from an indicator and a 'sell' signal from the price movement, you must employ other indicators or time frames until your signals are confirmed.

Another thing to keep in mind is to never lose sight of your trading strategy. Your rules for trading should always be implemented when using indicators.

www.ingramcontent.com/pod-product-compliance
Lightning Source LLC
LaVergne TN
LVHW052319060326
832902LV00023B/4493